Collection of Dog Poetry:

Poems About Dogs
Vol III

N. K. Hasen

Collection of Dog Poetry: Poems About Dogs Vol III

ISBN: 978-1-7337994-4-7

To Chelsey, who was the best friend I ever had and my first poetry muse. I will miss you dearly.

Table of Contents

Outside with Dog

Even More Dog Random

Poetry Written By Dog

A Dog's Poem

I am a dog
Trying to write poem
Short words I write
For paws I have
Makes it hard to write
I am dog
Who, wait a squirrel,
Where was I
I am a dog
Can't write anymore
Owner please,
Take over my poem now

A Dog's Poem 2

I, dog here
Write words
Which are
Short, simple poem
And this is my poetry:
Woof, woof woof bark
Woof bark bark bark, awoooo
Bark, bark woof woof grrr
Grrr woof bark bark woof awoooo.
As you can see human
I can write and speak poetry too.

🐾 🐾 🐾 🐾

Another Dog Poem

I begin my poem with:
Awwwooo awwoooooo ruff ruff.

Then a line of:
Bark bark bark grrr ruff.

Next comes a:
Woof bark woof bark awoooo!

Follow by:
Ruff ruff grrr grrr bark.

Next line some more:
Awoooo ruff awoooooo awoooo bark.

Then finish with:
Woof woof ruff ruff bark awoooo!

That is another poem by me, the dog
I wrote it for my owner who I love so much.

Dog Wrote Another Poem

Woof, woof, I am writing again.
A poem that's short and will rhyme.
Bark out my words on the dime.
I'll try to write with this pen.
Aroooo, this is too much,
Rhyming is too hard for me.
Hold on I might have a flea.
I scratch my fur as such.
Ah, all is good I continue to write.
Woof, bark I can't do this anymore.
I am glad I have an owner I adore.
To write poems that excite.

Dog's Favorite Poetry Form To Write

I write poetry
Using my favorite form
for a dog to use

Me, dog says Haiku
Are short, easy, fun lines which
Only are three lines

I, dog have a book
One hundred five dog haikus
Which I wrote about

A Dog Love Sonnet

What gives my furry heart to start to beat?
My four paws patter to your open arms
With happy grin my mouth hangs open to greet
For now, you are home; I put on my charms

Shall I cuddle close or push you away
You give me bounding love; I return same
Walks abound every day; there's also play
Alas, wasn't this way before you came

For I was found wandering streets alone
On cold December day you came for me
Brought me to your place; I now call my own
Have you now wrapped around my paw you see

Thou art my best friend till my final end
Saying my good-bye will be hard to send

Dog's Ode To Stuff Toy

My toy I love you so much
You are there when I awake
And you are there when I sleep
I enjoy your squeak you make
Your high pitch excites me
To the point I zoom around
And round the home
I love to chomp on you;
I am glad you don't mind
My teeth clamp on
Shake you from side to side
I love the runs we do together
As I race with you in mouth
You are my friend; my playmate;
When human owner goes to work
I am glad you are still with me
Regardless of some missing tuff.

🐾 🐾 🐾 🐾

Dog Take on Writing A Dizain

Can a dog write a Dizain you may ask?
Trying to count ten syllables is hard.
Why did owner give such demanding task?
I would rather be sniffing around yard.
Don't they know I'm not some poetry bard?
I can't even read to find words to rhyme.
Probably finish right before bedtime.
I will think of way for owner payback.
Less lines left I will finish this on time.
I am done and will eat my biscuit snack.

Dog Trying To Blog

I try to use paws... Difficult with small key buttons on...
Why can't they make large buttons for... call a computer?
I, dog have hard... with this device. I press... more than
one... comes on screen. They said easier... pen or pencil in
my... or paws. I will stop... random letters are appearing...
makes no sense. Blogging is taking... necessary for me
with... I have been typing away. I'll let owner... fine tooth
comb to make sure... correct and fix my post.

🐾 🐾 🐾 🐾

Cura, Sodales Iam Abiissent*

And I Knew A Dog Named Lucy

And I knew a dog named Lucy;
And she was the first dog I got to see;
And she would be my growing-up companion for as long as
she lived to be.
And she and I would play the day away when I was young.
And I used to pull her tail,
And she never minded at all.
And she would wait by the door when I came home from
school.
And she would look at you with her expressive eyes,
And you wonder how much she knew.
And I could talk to her,
And she kept any secrets I would tell her.
And I remember if I was crying, she would be right there to
comfort.
And she was the family dog which everyone loved.
And she had the sweetest temperament of any dog I knew.
And she watched us kids as we reached towards high
school.
And she loved us unconditionally,
And we loved her back even more.
And she was fourteen when she was taken.
And we mourned what a great dog we had.
And we kept her ashes, which lie out back,
And under pine tree buried in a box.
And still to this day I think of her,
And glad she helped me find my love of dogs.
And she will always be in my heart for ever more.

II.

For I Will Consider My Dog Chelsey

For I will consider my dog Chelsey.
For she is my loyal companion and best friend.
For under my roof she lives with me quietly waiting for her favorite activities to do.
For she is a great window watcher laying down by sliding glass doors waiting for those activity words to be heard.
For once she hears one of those words, she will stand upon all four paws looking at me in earnest.
For when at that moment she will stretch her forward paws and then her back to get ready to go.
For also she will let a rolling yawn come out of her mouth, her pink tongue coming out and then shake her whole body indicating she is ready.
For first activity of enjoyment are walks in morning and evening before sunset.
For I strap harness around her body, then clip leash, her eyes dance with excitement.
For once outside she will swagger her walk going around neighborhood; stopping sometimes to sniff.
For she will go out in all types of weather be it beautiful, snow, rain, humid or cold.
For second word of activity is meal time where twice a day she is fed.
For hearing the kibble go into the bowl; she is there in a blink of an eye waiting; eyeing her food.
For I have to give her a release word so she doesn't inhale her food too fast.
For next activity is playtime.

16

For she will run around the room; zooming fast.
For also it may involve a stuff toy that has her attention as she shakes it in her mouth, letting the squeaking be heard with delight in her eyes.
For another activity sometimes amuses her is taking photos of her in different settings.
For she has a smile that I capture with my camera.
For she will give different expressions every time I snap a picture.
For she knows she will get something in return; normally a treat or two.
For she will tolerate the dressing up; the hats; the bandanas and glasses too.
For she will probably think she is star which is true.
For I have many prints and wall decor of her everywhere in my rooms.
For her last activity of enjoyment, she considers her favorite.
For she learns and practices over and over again until sometime without telling her she will do it from heart.
For they involve commands that always leads to treats at the end.
For she will sit then stay with perfection until she can't hold and want to do the next command without hesitation.
For sometimes I have repeat so she can pay attention to my signals both verbal and by hand.
For next command to look at me and then lay down and wait as I move closer to the finally act.
For I will place treats on her paws and say leave it as she looks at me smiling; waiting with a happy drooling doggy grin for the release of the word to eat her treats.

For once that word is spoken, she wastes no time devouring those treats; crumbs and all until nothing remains left.

For these activities are her favorite and brings our bond closer than ever.

For she is my loyal companion and best friend in a furry coat who loves me no matter what activities we do together.

🐾 🐾 🐾 🐾

III.

I Miss You, My Dog, So Much

I miss you, my dog, so much
I miss your smile which brighten my days.
I miss your zooming around rooms at top speed.
I miss hearing your jingling collar.
I miss you licking my hands.
I miss the way you would pout.
I miss your stubborn look you gave when outside on our walks.
I miss our walks outside; you and me in all types of weather.
I miss petting your soft fur; gave me calming times.
I miss seeing you in your spot near window; watching what was going on.
I miss seeing you when I would come home from work.
I miss seeing you cozy and comfy on your bed.
I miss taking you to grandma's house; she loved you so much too.
I miss our outings to pet stores; calming you when you were nervous especially for bath time there.
I miss seeing you on stair landing; your favorite area to sleep.
I missing hearing the gnawing of your antler you would gnaw away on it for hours.
I miss hearing squeaks as you played with your many toys.
I miss taking photos of you and dressing you up in costumes.
I miss putting bandanas on you for you had so many to choose from.

I miss your presence in my home; for you were everywhere in one position or another.
I will miss you; but you will be in my heart always.

🐾 🐾 🐾 🐾

IV.

For I Will Remember My Dogs

For I will remember my dogs I had in my life.
For they were my best friends and closest confidants.
For each one had their own unique gifts they offered.
For one was like a sibling to me when growing up with
eyes that seem to understand every word I say.
For I would tell her everything as she would keep the secrets.
For her brown eyes were most expressive and her gentle
nature she would comfort me when I was blue.
For we play many games as we grew up together.
For she would be there when I got home from school.
For she was part of my young life growing up.
For I had the best fourteen years learning from her
which opened my heart to other animals?
For now, she has passed from this world to the beyond.
For I had to wait twelve years for another dog to enter my
life.
For it was winter time when she came; shy and scared.
For she grew out her shell to be best dog I could ever had.
For she taught me how to be pet parent for she was the first
one I ever owned.
For she brought my confidence up when out with her walking
around town.
For we both had some similarities as we were both unsure
and quiet; preferring to stay home; not be around large
noises and crowds.
For that we bonded close; my best friend she will always be.
For she was also like a child to me;
For I worried about her in her final months she was still
living.

For I didn't know what I would do without her.
For she opened two doors of hobbies for me to try;
photography and poetry writing.
For I found two things I didn't know I would be good at;
she helped me hone my two hobby crafts.
For now, I have published a few poetry books which some
were related to inspiration from her.
For photography she became my model;
For she had a smile that radiated like the sun; not caring
what modeling props she would be wearing.
For she gave me an outlet for my creativity to blossom.
For her photos of her have been in magazines, exhibits,
greeting cards and calendars.
For she became sick after an accident;
For too quickly a few months later she passed from this
world leaving me to grief my first own pet I ever had.
For she will always be with me forever;
For I will remember my dogs which taught me so much
and opened many doors for me.
For they were the best friends I will always have and
For them they will help me find another when time is right.
For dogs will always be a part of my life for a very long time.

*Note: These four poems are put together into four parts in remembering two of my furry friends that had a big impact on my life. I decided to put the title in latin. Cura, Sodales Iam Abiissent loosely means "Beloved Friends Now Gone". First two words Cura, Sodales means roughly beloved friends and Iam Abiissent roughly means now gone. I used Google Translate to translate but it wasn't giving me correct translation when doing whole phrase.

Grieving, Memories and Remembering

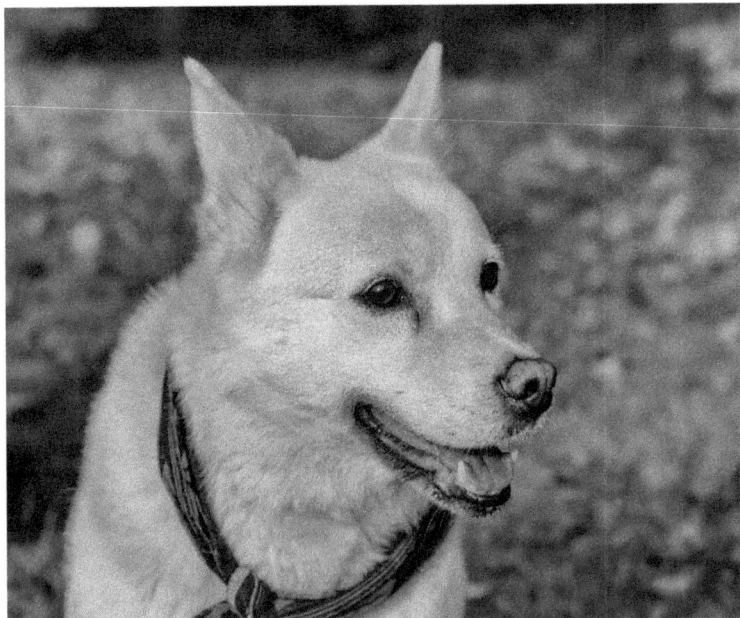

What To Do Now That You're Gone

What to do now that you're gone?
You gave me support by being here.
Your fur as I petted; comforted me when I was down.
You were the one to keep me going.
I am lost without you.
My days run into a blur.
One after another they melt into water.
I walk in a daze with no direction.
I need you back to help me again.
Sadness rules my time.
What do I do now that you are gone?
My best furry friend I miss you too much.

To Think You Are Really Gone

The jingling of the collar has stopped
Clicking of nails on kitchen floor have gone silent
The zooming around has disappeared
A bed lies empty; blanket folded with a collar on top
No open tongue out with happy grin to greet me
Waving tail has stopped its swooshing from side to side
The licking of fingers, hand and face are gone
Emptiness fills the rooms where you once were
My mind goes numb in deep sadness
To think that you are really gone from this world
I feel so alone now without you
I wish to see, hear and feel you once more.

🐾 🐾 🐾 🐾

Where To Find Dog Poetry Inspiration

My inspiration of writing has elapsed.
My partner, my furry friend now gone.
She gave me ideas of writing;
She let my creativity soar.
Just watching her; her actions
I put into words to write my poems.
Whether my voice or her voice
Poems poured out on paper.
She inspired my writing to new heights.
Where will I find my dog inspiration
Now that you are gone from this world?

No One To Greet Me

Stair landing is empty when I arrive home.
No one waiting; smiling at me waving their bushy tail.
Only a stuffed snowman sits in corner;
Branch arms up in greeting.
He will stay out for one more month, till he is put away.
Silence, no noise I hear when I get home.
No dog speaking, "I'm glad to see you!"
I trudge slowly up; silence is only there to greet me.
An empty void fills the home.
No one to greet me when I get home.

🐾 🐾 🐾 🐾

Not In Usual Spot

I went into bedroom
looking for
my dog, Chelsey,
but
She was not there
in usual spot
on bed;
until
I realized
that she had passed
from this world
as I wanted to
pet her fur
for I had
missed
stroking her every evening.

🐾 🐾 🐾 🐾

Where's Your Smiling Face

Where's your smiling face?
I saw it greet me every day.
From your bed your smiling face was there
Saying good morning let's get going.
You would thump your tail in morning greeting;
After you would stretch and yawn.
Your smile would send me off as I went to work.
Return I would open door; you standing on stair landing;
Your tail wagging, smiling down at me.
You would smile when photos were taken;
Such a model and a natural.
When you raced around; you'd stopped and smile;
Then continue on with your zooming run.
How I miss your gorgeous smile of yours
Which you brighten up my life.

Your Face Is Everywhere

I see your face everywhere.
Your early portrait hangs on wall
tongue out showing your happy grin.
An image cube; I turn and turn ever so often
with changing of seasons.
You smile from metals prints
placed on mantle;
With three photos of your last photo shoot.
You smile out of my current painting
I painted of you; an older version than the last.
You smile from greeting cards I get from Grandma.
Canvas photo of you on beach towel;
Smile with sunglasses on; perch from top of couch.
Mini painting, I have tried painting of you
dot my window sills view.
You are there in my photo frames
in living room where I pass by.
You smile at me from bedroom;
From a wood print block.
Your face is everywhere
It gives me comfort to know
I will not forget my best furry friend.

🐾 🐾 🐾 🐾

The Right Dog

I had glanced in your cage.
No noise you made; you looked sad.
Others barked out wanted the attention.
I looked closer to you.
You looked right back.
I jotted your number down;
So, I could check you out better.
Were you the right dog for me?

Now I see you were happy.
Tail wagging from side to side.
Mouth was open in a grin.
You would come near me;
Wanting your daily petting.
You were my constant companion;
Who enjoyed a better life.
You were the right dog for me!

A Smile

Her first by phone she wouldn't have a smile.
Her stoic face showed shy, nervous dog. A smile
I would try to coax her. Through loving patience, she
emerged to find a smile.
Many years I would take her picture and say give me a
smile.
Camera would come out with treats in hand; she would
give a smile.
Even with no camera she would give a smile.
When I would come home; she would be waiting with a
smile.
No more coaxing it came naturally; she had a smile.
No shy, scare dog who came from shelter. A smile
now would hang upon her face. She radiated in a smile
I would take with me until she passed. For a smile
would be her remembering mark as I know she looks down
with a smile.

Zooming Dog Haiku Sonnet

Dog standing in hall
Flashing a big doggy grin
She ready to spring

To run back and forth
From one room to another
At very top speeds

Smiling, mouth open
To stair landing; back again
Around furniture

She would zoom around
Happy pup with energy
Now there is no more

I miss zooming of my dog
Brought smile to my face

Miss Going Out In Winter With Dog

My companion,
I wish you were here
To see snow falling out there.
Your favorite time of year
For your coat was made for it.
I would take you out
You would eat snow
Enjoying a fresh treat;
Then run rocket dog
Up and down and around
On large lawn across the street.
Oh, how I will miss our winter together.
You and me outside
Whether blizzard, ice or cold
We would waddle through snow together.

I look at your picture

wishing you would jump out;
nudge my arm with a:
"I want you to pet me now!"

For I want to pet you again
as I miss stroking my fingers
along your fluffy fur coat.

The feel of smooth fur
which gave me strength
when I needed it most of all.

How I miss your fur
which I loved to
place my face against
to find comfort in
your double furry coat.

But you don't jump out
as I long to be with you again.

Memorial Tribute Lies On Dresser

Stuff pink purple pig lies alone with purple collar on top of fancy wooden box with dog's name etched gleaming bright with a lock which contains her ashes lies atop a dresser.

🐾 🐾 🐾 🐾

Memories of A Best Friend: My Dog Chelsey

Before holidays she passed from this world.
Sleeping in her walking outfit ready for a walk.
I miss four paws padding their way from room to room.
A walk schedule drawn to a halt; no dog to take outside.
Collar lies on an empty bed; no dog to hear jingling of tags.
Tears for one I really miss now on a cold lonely night.
I cuddled her one last time before she parted;
As I pictured her pushing me away with a paw;
No cuddles she liked at all.
She rests in peace her journey now done.
No more pictures of her; showing her gorgeous grin
The dog model has left the building in style with a scarf;
Her tail curled as she left me with many pictures and
memories.
How I miss every inch of you; wishing to pet you once
more.

Ten long years we were together.
You pulled me through my ups and down.
Gave me your fur for me to pet; when needed comfort.
You made me laugh as you zoomed around from room to
room;
Sometime with a stuff toy in your mouth.
Even when you were a senior you enjoy your toys.
Your smile always brightened my gloomy days.
Our walks were always entertaining;
Whether or not of what animals we would encounter and
chase.
You were silent; showed your love in many ways.
Going out; everyone commented on how pretty you were.

You were the one to get me out of the home more.
I will remember you my friend forever
Through many photos and writings, I have done of you.
And will continue into the future.

With having you in my life; I will be ready when time is right
To bring another pup into my home.
You gave me time and patience with being my first dog I ever owned.
For I learned from you as you learned from me,
I know now how to love another animal more than before.
Another one will come; maybe you will even help choose;
For you know which one will mend a broken heart.
To make me whole and happy again.
I will always miss you, my best friend, the first you will always be
You just wait in heaven and someday I will see you again soon.

🐾 🐾 🐾 🐾

Outside with Dog

Night Run On Cold Night

Pup with booties
Runs back and forth
In snow so deep
Paws not frozen
This cold winter night.

Trudge Along In Snow

Snow sprays my face
I trudge forward slowly
Snow is too deep
I try to keep pace
Dog is bounding quickly
Until she stops to sniff
Grabs a bite of snow
She plunges forward like nothing
As I lumber along
Trying to catch up to her
On a snowy, cold day.

🐾 🐾 🐾 🐾

It's Cold Outside

It's cold outside
I want to stay in
Dog needs to go out now.

It's cold outside
I want to stay buried under blankets
Dog will not let me be.

It's cold outside
Dog has business to do now!

🐾 🐾 🐾 🐾

Stoic Dog Won't Budge

Dog looks at me: stoic
Will not budge from spot
She stares at me
As I tug leash
To get her to move
For it is too cold outside

Enjoying Fresh Breezes

Windows down fresh breezes come through
Hear wind rustle as we drive on highway
I glance to backseat for a moment
Her snout raises in air
Look of awe with eyes closed
She soaks up scents in air
She pauses, looks at me with doggy smile
As if to say thank you for putting windows down
Now would you mind driving longer
For I am enjoying the breezes right now

Dog Sniffing Around

Dog walking around.
Head down. Sniff, sniff.
Smells fill the snout.
More snuffles into grass.
She categorizes her smells.
This one a new dog in neighborhood.
Oh, and this is my friend, Toffee.
And here is the lingering smell of squirrel.
Sigh, he gone now and can't be chased.
Here is the dog that growls at me all the time.
She lifts her snout.
Sniffs the air. There is a dog near.
Who could it be?
She moves forward. I follow.
To see who is up ahead.

🐾 🐾 🐾 🐾

Dog Dislike Traffic

Cars wiz by quickly
Zooming pass as dog and I walk
Down sidewalk I am unfazed
My dog stops; looks around
Sound of traffic too loud for her ears
She doesn't enjoy high sounds
Her mouth quivers as she turns head
I coax her on to our destination
She finally follows as I lead the way

🐾 🐾 🐾 🐾

Humid Short Walk

Summer heat rises
Pavement hot to touch
Paws walk the path
Pads thick help in walk
Must keep walk short
For humid outside
Will enjoy inside
Where AC keeps me cool.

Wearing Shades

Down street I walk
One cool dog wearing shades
Passersby stop to marvel
Why one keeps them on?
I enjoy wearing them
I don't mind at all
Keeps sun out of my eyes
And give others a big smile

Even More Dog Random

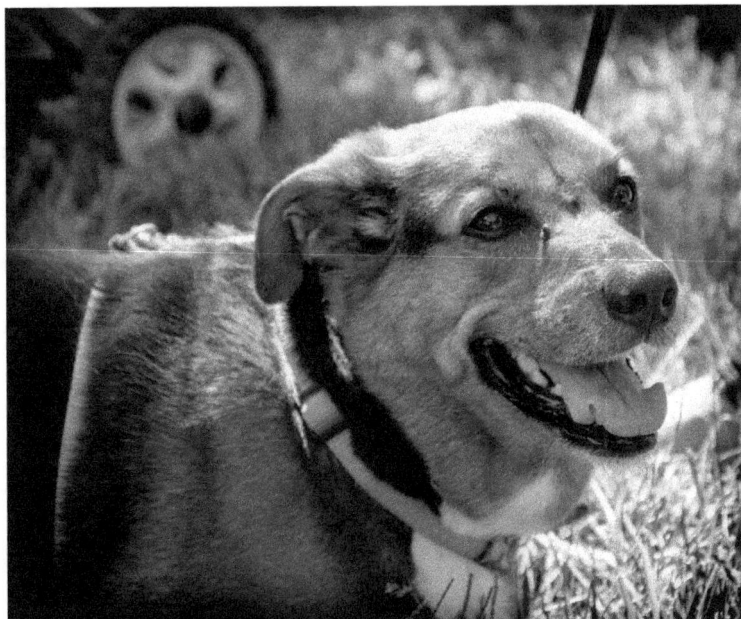

Dogs Are Love

Dogs are love
As they
Smile at you
Waving their tail.
They love unconditionally
Despite some of
Their hardships in life.
They are full of wonder
Which makes it hard
When they pass on
For they share a strong bond
With whoever has
Brought them into their home.

A Fur Friend's Job

My friend unfortunately doesn't have job.
She has been unemployed all her life.
She stays at home;
Sleeping every chance, she gets.
To say she has a profession;
Would be to underscore the meaning.
For she window watches and play,
When she is not involved in sleeping.
But her job is to love unconditionally her owner.
Her smile, softens the bad days.
She licks her encouragement.
She brings enjoyment in the home
With her sometimes-crazy ways.
I realize she is lucky to not work
But days can be boredom with nothing to do.
For a dog's life is simple at its best,
Just relaxing at home and doing things at your own pace.

🐾 🐾 🐾 🐾

Dog's Take On Halloween

What's up with weird costumes you wear once a year
Some are scary and look too funny on you
Why do you always want to put one on me too
Those bags smell good; I wish you would open one bag for
me
But you nudge me away, saying they're bad for me
You worry what would happen if I eat them
And why does doorbell ring almost every minute
I bark; you hush me as you open door
Little voices shout: trick or treat
You grab a big bowl now with candies
And pass a few out as I watch with envy
Wishing I could grab those treats for myself
Alas, the Halloween decorations are too out of reach
For I would like to get a hold of them
And you told me, I had to wait to do my business until
after eight o'clock
I'm trying my best after woofing down Halloween biscuit
and lapping tons of water
Will these two hours never end
Wake me up when this holiday is gone

🐾 🐾 🐾 🐾

Dogs On Other Side Of Fence

I hear dogs bark on other side of fence.
They bark with joy of playing.

I walk; peer over fence.
I see two dogs prancing around each other.

One bows, front paws down.
Other returns gesture.

They are off racing around yard.
In joy they voice their barks.

🐾 🐾 🐾 🐾

In Praise of My Dog

My dog does not write poems.
She unable to anyways; for she has
four paws with no way to hold a pen.
I guess if she did start; would have to use
her mouth to write. But, then the words
she knows is not that much.
They would probably be: sit, stay, watch,
treat, leave it, toy, outside and dog.
Neither does she read poems, even though
it looks like she does when she is having a photo taken
of her with a poetry book under paws.
She would rather sleep the day away.
She plays with toys she grabs
from toy box in bed room.
Zooms around the room; smiles a smile
with doggy grin to say:
OK, right now try to chase me around the room.
She is happy just lounging nearby me,
as I stroke her fur when watching TV.
She loves the walks; we go outside,
sniffs everything, she can find nearby.
She licks to show she loves you,
that is the way she communicates;
besides being a good listener too.
If she does write poems, they are in her head;
For I have not seen any pages lying about.
Her parents which I will never know,
never wrote poems, they have paws too.
My childhood dog was the same too,
no poems I saw, but intelligent eyes
stared out to give me pause;

that if she could, she would have something to say.
My dog inspires me to write;
her actions are what speak volumes
in poems I write about her.

🐾 🐾 🐾 🐾

My Dog Is A Child

My dog is a child
she clings to me
when she sees strangers.

She runs behinds me
peers around shy
not sure what to make of them.

She looks curiously on
looks to me for guidance.

I encourage her as she
takes tentative steps
to meet the stranger.

🐾 🐾 🐾 🐾

Staring Out Of Window

I walked into room
Saw you staring out:
Your dominion high above
On third level condo
Watching all that transpired
Under your focused gaze
You only took a quick glance
As I enter; then back to staring
Out of sliding glass window
Nothing escaped your notice
Until you were satisfied
Nothing would get passed your eyes;
Satisfied you finally took your nap

Waiting For Her Treat

She stands staring... Her eyes gaze longingly at... I see the counter where... A piece of her favorite... She smacks her... Does her tricks with... For she can be smart when... I see her eyeing what is now in... I say leave it while I give her command to... She watches... Drool starts to form as she is getting... snack is what she loves. On paws she is... eat what she really... I give nod to... Finally, with a look... Head down devours until... gone, with no crumbs left on... Where she continues to lick and... Then she looks up expecting... from me which will not happen.

🐾 🐾 🐾 🐾

Last Petting Of the Evening

Your strokes gentle upon my face
You rub your hand in my fur
I sit still
Take it all in
As each part gets stroke
I close my eyes enjoying the last petting of evening
I don't want it to end
But it will because it's time for bed

🐾 🐾 🐾 🐾

When Will You Come Home

I left my stuffed toy where it lies.
How can I play with it?
You leave me at Grandma's
   with a wave of your hand
      and a kiss on my snout.

I am helpless waiting for your return.
How could you leave me?
I am a dog, silent, not understanding
   what vacation means
      or when you will return to me.

I sigh, day and night.
Will you come back for me?
Front door opens,
   I see you there, I stare
      making sure it is finally you.

I am too overjoyed to get up.
I let you come to me
   and give you the
      I miss you lick
      as you pet my fur.

.

Dog Resting In Hallway

She lays blended on carpet floor, resting her head
between paws; eyes closed sleeping
in semi darken hallway.

🐾 🐾 🐾 🐾

Rumbling Storm Coming

I hear the rumbling far away.
My ears perk up; swivel back and forth.
What's that I hear so far away?
It is what I dislike the most.
Oh, how I hear it rumbling closer.
I will wander from room to room pacing back and forth;
I will seek out my owner to comfort me.
I try to remember where I left him.
I was sleeping peacefully upon my bed.
To living room, I go; he is not here.
I don't hear him in the kitchen.
Oh, where did my owner go?
I remember with dread he left for work early in the day.
Pace and whine wishing he was here.
Storm I hear is drawing near; darkness I see sliding over
Rooms become darker; I hear rumbling closer than ever.
I let out a whimper; only one place to go.
I head to the bathroom to get away.
But alas the noise is building.
I nudge the shower curtain just a little.
Place front paws up on tub I climb in managing not to fall.
My sanctuary; my place of refuge
It greets with a cold tub bottom.
I will ride out this storm till it ends.
I will stay here until I know I'm safe.
What's a dog to do with many windows in this place?
Only place the bathroom; no windows to show the storm.
I am safe for now; as I wait out this storm.

🐾 🐾 🐾 🐾

69

3600 Barkpoints

3600 barkpoints to go
Move one paw forward
Another paw to follow
Walk the circuit outside
2600 barkpoints left to go
Walk to kitchen for food
quick play here
Outside again for break
2200 barkpoints left to go
Play with toys
shake them around;
Run around with them
Stop to shake my head
Walk through rooms
Now 1600 barkpoints left to go
Another walk around
Paws covering ground
Quick stop to sniff
Resume down the stretch
Walk further than before
900 barkpoints left to go
Shake my head
Have owner pet here and there
Do tricks for a treat
Goal on fitbark almost there
Race around add some more
500 barkpoints only now
Last time out
Walk around and sniff
Business done; upstairs
In for drying paws

250 barkpoints only now
Walk to bedroom
Circle on bed around and around
settle in for sleep
But, wait for owner to pet me goodnight
Wait a minute; up again
Pace to owner's bed
Another pat; back I go to bed
Turn around once more
Shake my head
Settle in for bed
0 barkpoints to go
Until tomorrow repeat again
3600 barkpoints left to go

🐾 🐾 🐾 🐾

One Dog

One dog
Came into my life
Changed it
With just herself
Opening up
A door to explore
Possibilities
I would not have seen.

🐾 🐾 🐾 🐾

INDEX

About the Author

I am a poet, writer and amateur photographer who lives in Ohio. I have written eleven poetry books and one non-poetry book called, *Chelsey Loves To Read*, in tribute to my dog. My dog, Chelsey, who recently passed away inspired me in writing poetry and other writings. I have a poetry blog at poetrybyhasen.wordpress.com.

Other Books by N. K. Hasen

Poetry Books

Along a Trodden Path I Travel

Collection Of Dog Poetry: Poems About Dogs

Something Close At The Roots

30 Poems In 30 Days: April Poetry Challenge

110 Haiku Poems

Ode To Colors

30 Poems In 30 Days: April Poetry Challenge Vol. II

105 Dog Haikus

Collection Of Dog Poetry: Poems About Dogs Vol. II

Dog Double Elevenie

30 Poems In 30 Days: April Poetry Challenge Vol. III

Non-Poetry Books

Chelsey Loves To Read

www.ingramcontent.com/pod-product-compliance
Lightning Source LLC
Chambersburg PA
CBHW060140050426
42448CB00010B/2225